SHORT WALKS
MADE EASY

AVIEMOR
THE CAIRNGORMS

Ordnance
Survey

Contents

Getting outside in the Cairngorms 6

We smile more when we're outside 8

Respecting the countryside 11

Using this guide 12

Walk 1 Grantown-on-Spey **14**

Walk 2 Carrbridge **20**

Photos Scenes from the walks 26

Walk 3 Nethy Bridge **28**

Walk 4 Loch Garten and Loch
Mallachie **34**

Photos Wildlife interest 40

Walk 5 Aviemore to Boat of Garten **42**

Walk 6 Loch Morlich **48**

Walk 7 Dalraddy to Kincraig **54**

Photos Cafés and pubs 60

Walk 8 Loch an Eilein **62**

Walk 9 Kingussie **68**

Walk 10 Newtonmore **74**

Credits 80

Map symbols   Front cover flap

Accessibility and
    what to take   Back cover flap

Walk locations   Inside front cover

Your next adventure?   Inside back cover

Walk 1

GRANTOWN-
ON-SPEY

Distance
3.1 miles/5km

Time
1½ hours   CATCH A BUS

Start/Finish
Grantown-on-Spey

Parking PH26 3HH
Burnfield car park

Cafés/pubs
Grantown-on-Spey

**Interesting town
and glorious
pinewoods trail**

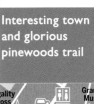

Page 14

The dog rose is a wild rose of hedgerows, woodland edges and scrubland. It has pretty, single-flowered blooms in June and bright red rose hips that ripen in autumn

Alder

Wood cranesbill

Wood pigeons are large, mainly grey birds whose wings make a loud clatter as they fly away. Their cooing call is a familiar sound in woodlands

Highland Folk Museum ☆ Loch Imrich   🖥 🍵 Balavil Hotel   4½ miles

3½ miles   **9**   4 miles

P
🚻
ℹ️

8 ▪ Keep **ahead** up lane then turn **left** to return along Main Street.

9 ▪ Optionally, 100 yards before Co-Op, turn **left** through gate and down steep path for circuit of Loch Imrich.

Publishing information

ISBN 978 0 319092 29 3
1st edition published by Ordnance Survey 2022.

www.ordnancesurvey.co.uk

While every care has been taken to ensure the accuracy of the route directions, the publishers cannot accept responsibility for errors or omissions, or for changes in details given. The countryside is not static: hedges and fences can be removed, stiles can be replaced by gates, field boundaries can alter, footpaths can be rerouted and changes in ownership can result in the closure or diversion of some concessionary paths. Also, paths that are easy and pleasant for walking in fine conditions may become slippery, muddy and difficult in wet weather.

If you find an inaccuracy in either the text or maps, please contact Ordnance Survey at os.uk/contact.

Milestone Publishing credits

Author: Felicity Martin

Series editor: Kevin Freeborn

Maps: Cosmographics

Design and Production: Patrick Dawson, Milestone Publishing

Printed in Malta by Gutenberg Press

Photography credits

Walk 2

CARRBRIDGE

Distance
1.75 miles / 2.8 km

Time
1 hour

Start/Finish
Carrbridge

Parking PH23 3AS
Village car park

Cafés/pubs
Carrbridge

Add Forest Adventure Park visit to beautiful walk

Page 20

Walk 3

NETHY BRIDGE

Distance
3.3 miles / 5.3 km

Time
1½ hours

Start/Finish
Nethy Bridge

Parking PH25 3DA
At Community Centre

Cafés/pubs
Nethy Bridge

Delightful riverside path and woodland trail

Page 28

Walk 4

LOCH GARTEN AND LOCH MALLACHIE

Distance
3.2 miles / 5.1 km

Time
1½ hours

Start/Finish
RSPB Loch Garten

Parking PH24 3BY
Loch Garten car park

Cafés/pubs
Hot drinks/snacks at Nature Centre shop

Visit in summer to watch for ospreys

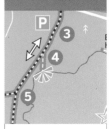

Page 34

Walk 5	Walk 6	Walk 7
AVIEMORE TO BOAT OF GARTEN	**LOCH MORLICH**	**DALRADDY TO KINCRAIG**

Walk 5	Walk 6	Walk 7
Distance 6 miles/9.7km	**Distance** 3.6 miles/5.8km	**Distance** 2.9 miles/4.7km
Time 2¾ hours *RETURN BY STEAM TRAIN*	**Time** 1¾ hours *CATCH A BUS*	**Time** 1½ hours *CATCH A BUS*
Start/Finish Aviemore/Boat of Garten	**Start/Finish** Glenmore	**Start/Finish** Dalraddy/Kincraig
Parking PH22 1RH Speyside Railway	**Parking** PH22 1QU Loch Morlich Beach	**Parking** PH22 1QB Dalraddy Holiday Park
Cafés/pubs Aviemore and Boat of Garten	**Cafés/pubs** Boathouse Café on beach	**Cafés/pubs** Café at start; cafés in Kincraig
Speyside Way ramble and steam train ride	**Scotland's highest beach; see Cairngorm reindeer**	**Wild mountain views and woodland bird song**

 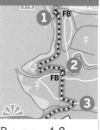 

Page 42	Page 48	Page 54

Walk 8

LOCH AN EILEIN

Distance
3.5 miles/5.6km

Time
1¾ hours

Start/Finish
Loch an Eilein

Parking PH22 1QP
Loch an Eilein

Cafés/pubs
None; nearest at
Inverdruie, 1 mile

Most beautiful
loch circuit and
island-castle ruin

Page 62

Walk 9

KINGUSSIE

Distance
3.6 miles/5.7km

Time
2 hours   GO BY TRAIN
CATCH A BUS

Start/Finish
Kingussie

Parking PH21 1EU
Ardvonie car park

Cafés/pubs
Kingussie

Military history,
shinty, a wooded
stream and
marshland vistas

Page 68

Walk 10

NEWTONMORE

Distance
4.5 miles/7.2km

Time
2¼ hours   GO BY TRAIN
CATCH A BUS

Start/Finish
Newtonmore

Parking PH20 1DZ
Glen Road car park

Cafés/pubs
Newtonmore

Wildcat Trail,
scenic Spey
meadows and
riverside wildlife

Page 74

Contents **5**

GETTING OUTSIDE IN THE CAIRNGORMS

"

Ancient
Caledonian
woodland,
beautiful lochs,
sparkling
riversides,
lush meadows
and, not to
be missed,
Scotland's
highest beach.

OS Champion
Eddie Fitzpatrick

Loch Morlich beach

A very warm welcome to the new Short Walks Made Easy guide to Aviemore and the Cairngorms – what a fantastic selection of leisurely walks we have for you along the Spey Valley!

The Cairngorms is Great Britain's most northerly national park, located in the Highlands of Scotland. It is also the largest – covering 1,750 square miles – and has some of the most rugged countryside in Great Britain.

While upland splendour forms magnificent snow-capped backdrops, all the routes in this guide are easy-going, low-level short walks. Ranging along the Spey Valley, from Grantown through Aviemore to Newtonmore, each splendid outing is set amid stunning scenery with a focus on ancient Caledonian woodland, beautiful lochs, sparkling riversides, lush meadows and, not to be missed, Scotland's highest beach at Loch Morlich.

Wildlife watching opportunities abound with a good chance of spotting red squirrels, crossbills and crested tits in the forests of Abernethy, observing ospreys at Loch Garten, and getting up close to reindeer at Glenmore.

Steam train enthusiasts can have a stroll and ride day out from Aviemore. Look out too for historic Dulnain Bridge at Carrbridge, take in the hilltop fortification of Ruthven Barracks from Kingussie, and the romantic island ruin of Loch an Eilein Castle.

Speyside has the greatest concentration of malt whisky producers in the world, so why not enjoy a touch of post-walk relaxation in sampling some fine Highland hospitality?

Eddie Fitzpatrick, OS Champion

WE SMILE MORE
WHEN WE'RE OUTSIDE

Anagach Woods, Grantown-on-Spey

Whether it's a short walk during our lunch break or a full day's outdoor adventure, we know that a good dose of fresh air is just the tonic we all need.

At Ordnance Survey (OS), we're passionate about helping more people to get outside more often. It sits at the heart of everything we do, and through our products and services, we aim to help you lead an active outdoor lifestyle, so that you can live longer, stay younger and enjoy life more.

We firmly believe the outdoors is for everyone, and we want to help you find the very best Great Britain has to offer. We are blessed with an island that is beautiful and unique, with a rich and varied landscape. There are coastal paths to meander along, woodlands to explore, countryside to roam, and cities to uncover. Our trusted source of inspirational content is bursting with ideas for places to go, things to do and easy beginner's guides on how to get started.

It can be daunting when you're new to something, so we want to bring you the know-how from the people who live and breathe the outdoors. To help guide us, our team of awe-inspiring OS Champions share their favourite places to visit, hints and tips for outdoor adventures, as well as tried and tested accessible, family and wheelchair-friendly routes. We hope that you will feel inspired to spend more time outside and reap the physical and mental health benefits that the outdoors has to offer. With our handy guides, paper and digital mapping, and exciting new apps, we can be with you every step of the way.

To find out more visit os.uk/getoutside

RESPECTING
THE COUNTRYSIDE

You can't beat getting outside in the Scottish countryside, but it's vital that we leave no trace when we're enjoying the great outdoors.

Let's make sure that generations to come can enjoy the countryside just as we do.

 Care for your environment

 Keep your dog under proper control

 Take responsibility for your own actions

 Respect people's privacy and peace of mind

 Take extra care if organising a group or event

 Help land managers and others to work safely and effectively

For more details please visit
www.outdooraccess-scotland.scot

Easy-to-follow National Park walks for everyone

Before setting off

Check the walk information panel to plan your outing

- Consider using **Public transport** where flagged. If driving, note the satnav postcode for the car park under **Parking**
- The suggested **Time** is based on a gentle pace
- Note the availability of **Cafés**, tearooms and pubs, and **Toilets**

Terrain and hilliness

- **Terrain** indicates the nature of the route surface
- Any rises and falls are noted under **Hilliness**

Walking with your dog?

- This panel states where **Dogs** must be on a lead and how many stiles there are – in case you need to lift your dog
- Keep dogs on leads where there are livestock and between April and August in forest where there are ground-nesting birds

A perfectly pocket-sized walking guide

- Handily sized for ease of use on each walk
- When not being read, it fits nicely into a pocket...
- ...so between points, put this book in the pocket of your coat, trousers or day sack and enjoy your stroll in glorious national park countryside – we've made it pocket-sized for a reason!

Flexibility of route presentation to suit all readers

- **Not comfortable map reading?** Then use the simple-to-follow route profile and accompanying route description and pictures
- **Happy to map read?** New-look walk mapping makes it easier for you to focus on the route and the points of interest along the way
- **Read the insightful Did you know?, Local legend, Stories behind the walk** and **Nature notes** to help you make the most of your day out and to enjoy all that each walk has to offer

The easy-to-use walk map

- **Large-scale** mapping for ultra-clear route finding

- **Numbered points** at key turns along the route that tie in with the route instructions and respective points marked on the profile

- **Pictorial symbols** for intuitive map reading, see Map Symbols on the front cover flap

The simple-to-follow walk profile

- Progress easily along the route using the illustrative profile, it has **numbered points** for key turning points and **graduated distance** markers

- Easy-read **route directions** with turn-by-turn detail

- Reassuring **route photographs** for each numbered point

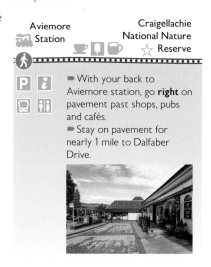

Many of the features and symbols shown are taken from Ordnance Survey's celebrated **Explorer** mapping, designed to help people across Great Britain enjoy leisure time spent outside. For more on this – and how you can start planning your own walks and adventures, please see the inside back cover.

GRANTOWN-ON-SPEY

With its wide streets and fine stone buildings it's difficult to believe that Grantown only has a population of about 2,000. It has long been a market centre for the surrounding countryside and a popular holiday destination. The square is the venue for the Grantown Hogmanay Street Party, one of the biggest Hogmanay gatherings in the Highlands. This walk starts by the museum and explores the Blue Trail around Anagach Woods, a haven for wildlife, including the endangered capercaillie.

Distance	3.1 miles/5km
Time	1½ hours
Start/Finish	Grantown-on-Spey Museum
Parking PH26 3HH	Burnfield car park
Public toilets	On High Street
Cafés/pubs	Grantown-on-Spey
Terrain	Pavement and gravel forest tracks/paths
Hilliness	No hills; short inclines
Dogs	Dogs welcome, keep on a short lead April to August to avoid disturbing capercaillie. No stiles
Footwear	Year round

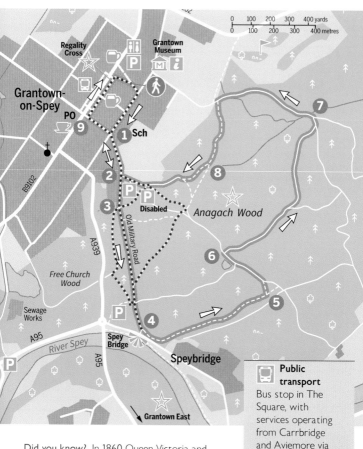

Did you know? In 1860 Queen Victoria and Prince Albert visited Grantown and stayed overnight at the Grant Arms Hotel, the grandest building in the town square.

On this route you will walk along Wade's Road, an 18th-century military road that runs through Anagach Woods. It is one of a network of roads built under the supervision of General George Wade, Commander-in-Chief of the British Forces. Completed in 1733, after the first Jacobite Rebellion, it was designed to provide the king's army fast travel through the region to enable them to subdue the Highland clans.

STORIES BEHIND THE WALK

Grantown Museum Don't miss a visit to Grantown Museum to learn about the history of the town, the Highland way of life and local wildlife. The planned village was established in 1765 by the local landowner, Sir James Grant. He laid it out around a large, central square on a site that was well served by two military roads. Outside the museum is a wooden bell tower or campanile, built to house the town bell that was originally used to call worshippers and alert people to the opening of the local shops.

☆ **Regailty Cross** Grantown was a busy community before the 18th-century stone buildings you see today were built. It was originally called Castletown of Freuchie, after the castle that was the seat of the Grant chiefs of Strathspey. In 1694 it was renamed when King William and Queen Mary granted it royal burgh status and declared that a market cross should be erected. Called the Regality Cross, it was used for proclamations and punishments.

Grantown Museum | Anagach ☆ Wood

½ mile | River Sp

➤ Walk **downhill** from museum; turn **right** at junction signed River Spey Forest Walks.
➤ Continue to Grantown Primary School.

① ➤ Pass school and turn **left** at crossroads by Fire Station, signed Anagach Woodland Walks.

② ➤ At parking area and information boards keep **ahead** on gravel lane, signed Woodland Walks All Routes, to gate.

☆ Anagach Wood

Although appearing entirely natural, Anagach Wood was first planted in 1766 with Scots pine, birch and oak. Before then this area was known as the Moor of Grant-town. Today the wood is largely naturally regenerated with self-seeded trees of mixed ages, including a few of the original trees. It is rich in wildlife, including many of the rarer species found in ancient pinewoods. The ridges in the wood are glacial moraines, deposited in the last Ice Age.

☆ Grantown East

The railway line that served Grantown only lasted from 1863 to 1968. The derelict railway station is now the East Highland Heritage and Cultural Centre, which has a gift shop and the Revack Mini Railway. Here you can view short videos about the Speyside Line, Kilt Making, Grantown East Tartan, Highland Games and Clydesdale Horses. The restaurant, situated in two classic dining cars, is famed for its pizzas, including a range of unique sweet Puddin' Pizzas.

Grantown East Highland Heritage and Cultural Centre
☆ (½ mile)

1 mile

3 ➡ Pass gate and stay **ahead-left** on main trail (Old Military Road).
➡ Keep **ahead** over two junctions to reach barrier (on right).

4 ➡ By barrier onto road fork **left**. (For River Spey view, fork **right** round barrier, cross lane and head down steps.)
➡ Zigzag **uphill** above Speybank and follow main path along ridge to reach blue- and red-ringed post.

1½ miles

5 ➡ At post turn **left**, downhill.
➡ At bottom turn **left** at T-junction and keep **ahead** past bench and pond to next junction.

NATURE NOTES

By the time the Spey reaches Grantown and flows past Anagach Woods it is a broad, strong river. Most of the woods are Scots pine and provide habitat for rare capercaillie. Other parts have broadleaved trees, such as goat willow and wych elm. The woods grow on relatively infertile soil, but there is better agricultural land in the surrounding countryside.

Conical brittlestem fungi grow in clusters from rotting wood and glisten beautifully after rain

The speckled wood flies in partially shaded woodland with dappled sunlight. Unlike most other butterflies its numbers are increasing

⑦
2 miles

6 ➤ Go **right**, uphill.
➤ Keep **left** at bench where lesser path forks right and walk on to wide junction.

7 ➤ Turn **left** at junction (signed Grantown) and join Speyside Way.
➤ Just before golf course turn **left**, still on Speyside Way, cross two streams and continue to fork.

Scotland's native elm, the wych elm, has been decimated by Dutch elm disease. It regenerates well and can be found in woods and beside streams

Ling is a type of heather

Violets have heart-shaped leaves that are food for the caterpillars of fritillary butterflies

Anagach Wood ☆

2½ miles

Disabled
P car park

Regality
Cross ☆

Grantown
Museum
🏛

9

3 miles

8 ▸ Branch **right** to cross open area then later pass gate and disabled car park.
▸ Turn **right** at junction 2 and keep **ahead** over crossroads at 1 towards The Square.

9 ▸ Turn **right** by pedestrian crossing to return past cafés and pubs to reach Regality Cross.
▸ Here, turn **right** down to car park and museum.

WALK 2

CARRBRIDGE

Carrbridge – sometimes written as Carr-bridge – is a planned village whose blueprint was drawn up in 1808. By then it had a second 'new' bridge to carry wheeled traffic over the river. Only an inn and some crofts were here until the Aviemore to Inverness railway line opened in 1898, after which it grew as a holiday village. Set in glorious and very accessible countryside, pinewoods bring nature right up to the houses. This walk uses a network of waymarked trails.

Distance	1.75 miles/2.8km
Time	1 hour
Start/Finish	Carrbridge
Parking PH23 3AS	Carrbridge car park
Public toilets	Carrbridge car park
Cafés/pubs	Along main street in Carrbridge
Terrain	Pavement, forest paths and quiet lanes
Hilliness	Riverside trail is flat, short inclines on forest paths

 **Dogs**
Dogs welcome under close control or on leads. No stiles

Footwear
Year round

Public transport

Train services operate on the Perth to Inverness line, with railway station accessed from ③ on the walk. Bus stop in the car park, with services operating from Inverness, Grantown-on-Spey and Aviemore www.stagecoachbus.com

Accessibility

Pushchair accessible throughout. Riverside Walk is wheelchair accessible; at ③, wheelchairs should return left along pavement to road bridge then right back to car park

Did you know? The Old Packhorse Bridge was built because funeral processions heading to the Church of Duthil for burial were often delayed because it was impossible to ford the River Dulnain when in spate. The Grant Clan Chief commissioned the construction, which was paid for out of parish stipends.

Local legend There are many stories of a large black cat haunting the Highlands. It was called the Cat Sith and believed to be a fairy creature or a witch. The legends surrounding this apparition appear to have been inspired by the black Kellas cat, a cross between a domestic cat and a wildcat.

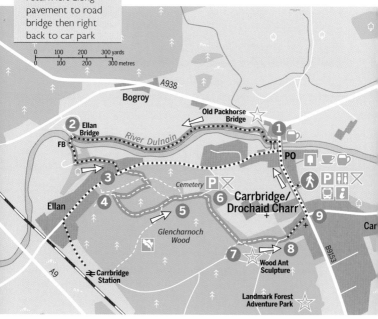

STORIES BEHIND THE WALK

☆ **Old Packhorse Bridge** Carrbridge's iconic packhorse bridge was built in 1717. It is a graceful single arch spanning the River Dulnain and is best seen from the road bridge at **❶** or the bench just before this, where steps descend to the river bank. Its parapets and side walls were badly damaged by floods, giving it the precarious appearance it has today.

☆ **Landmark Forest Adventure Park** Occupying a large area of forest just south of this walk, Landmark is one of the major attractions in Cairngorms National Park. A visit makes a great family day out. The rides and trails offer fun and activity for children of all ages. They range from a tropical Butterfly House and Dinosaur Kingdom to the thrills of the Wildwater Coaster and Tarzan Trail.

☆ Old Packhorse Bridge

➠ From car park entrance turn **right** along Carrbridge's main street, past Cairn Hotel, Coffee Shop, Artist's Studio and Spar shop towards the river.

❶ ➠ Cross bridge over River Dulnain and immediately go **left** on path signed Riverside Walk.
➠ The path joins a gravel lane, which soon narrows to a path. Follow it to next bridge.

☆ Chainsaw carving

Local chainsaw sculptors Alice and Jeff Buttress were heavily involved in the Scottish Chainsaw Carving Competition, which started in Carrbridge in 2003. They created the wooden carving of the Old Packhorse Bridge by the start point to celebrate its 300th anniversary. Local creatures such as osprey, capercaillie, deer and red squirrel are represented on the pillars. You will spot many other works of theirs on this walk.

◪ Glencharnoch and Ellan Woods

Owned by the Woodland Trust, Glencharnoch Wood is a significant area of ancient woodland, particularly rich in the species that inhabit remnants of Caledonian forest. Rare crested tits and Scottish crossbills are found here, as well as endangered flora, such as creeping lady's tresses, a beautiful wild orchid. Glencharnoch is part of Ellan Wood, the large pinewood fringing the village.

½ mile   ➋ Ellan Bridge

➋ ➼ At footbridge, where blue arrow on post points left, **cross** river.
➼ Shortly, at arrow for Village, turn **left** along a lane and follow it to road junction.

➌ ➼ At road go diagonally **left** across it and up path signed Glencharnoch Wood Walk.
➼ At next fingerpost keep **left** signed Cemetery then take next path **right** (unsigned).

NATURE NOTES

Glencharnoch Wood has enormous biodiversity value and contains many endangered and rare species. A pinewood rarity, the crested tit, is fairly common here, as are Scottish crossbills and redstarts. Several wildflowers that are key indicators of ancient pinewood grow here, including chickweed wintergreen and the rare orchid, creeping lady's tresses. Wood ant nests appear as orange mounds against the green ground foliage of heather, cowberry and blaeberry.

Barn owls have a tough time this far north, but can be seen hunting low over open country, riverbanks and roadside verges

Scotch argus butterfly

Glencharnoch Wood | Cemetery

4 ➤ Turn **left** at next junction, following green arrow on post.
➤ At fingerpost keep **ahead**, signed Station Road 350 yards, ignore left turn and pass below small carved barn owl.
➤ Continue to cemetery.

1 mile

5 ➤ At fingerpost by cemetery keep **ahead**, signed Station Road 250 yards, into woodland car park.

6 ➤ By walks and wood ants information boards in car park turn sharp **right**, signed Main Street ½ mile.
➤ Keep **left** at next junction (yellow arrow), ignore side turns keeping **forward** to next fingerpost.

Shaggy inkcap fungi have tall, white, shaggy caps. As they age, the gills turn black and the cap gradually dissolves from the rim

Gorse is a spiny evergreen shrub with yellow flowers that colonises rough open spaces

Chickweed wintergreen, also known as 'Arctic starflower', has a preference for northern climes

P
✕
6

Wood ant
sculpture ☆

7

Landmark Forest Adventure ☆
Park (375 yards)

8 •••••••••• **9** ••••••••••••••••••

1½ miles

P **□**
♿ **✕**
i

7 ➤ Keep **left** at next fingerpost: Main Street 300 yards. (Large wood ant sculpture 40 yards to right.)
➤ Beyond another fingerpost to Main Street, path curves **left** to green gate.

8 ➤ Pass gate.
➤ Follow lane to road by Village Hall.

9 ➤ Turn **left** then first **right** back into car park.

Opposite (clockwise): Ellan, Carrbridge;
The Cairngorms from Loch Morlich;
Loch Insh church, Dalraddy; Loch Morlich
This page (clockwise): Lairig Ghru;
Gynack Burn, Kingussie; River Dulnain,
Nethy Bridge

WALK 3

NETHY BRIDGE

The peaceful village of Nethy Bridge lies midway between Aviemore and Grantown-on-Spey, but is easily missed if you stay on A-roads. It is situated about a mile upstream from where the River Nethy joins the Spey. This beautiful walk follows King's Road trail, which starts along the pretty River Walk before entering Dell Woods, an outstanding example of native pinewood.

Distance	3.3 miles/5.3km
Time	1½ hours
Start/Finish	Nethy Bridge car park
Parking PH25 3DA	Community Centre car park (donation)
Public toilets	Community Centre
Cafés/pubs	Nethy House café; Nethy Bridge Hotel
Terrain	Riverside and woodland paths; one set of steps
Hilliness	No hills; fairly level
Dogs	Dogs welcome on leads. No stiles
Footwear	Year round

Did you know? The original settlement here was known as Abernethy and consisted of scattered small farms (crofts). Gradually the village coalesced around the bridge and became known as Nethy Bridge. Because it is so closely allied to the Abernethy Forest it has adopted the name 'The Forest Village'.

The King's Road, the track from **8** back into Nethy Bridge, was built in the 13th century following a royal decree that communications be improved between the village and Tulloch to the south. At one time it would have rung to the sound of carts carrying timber and farm products.

Public transport

Bus stop near start, with services operating from Grantown-on-Spey and Aviemore via Boat of Garten, www.stagecoachbus.com. Broomhill Station (Strathspey Railway) 1½ miles away, www.strathspeyrailway.net

Accessibility

■■■■■■■■■■

Suitable for pushchairs throughout (with one set of steps); River Walk, King's Road and Birch Wood circular suitable for wheelchairs

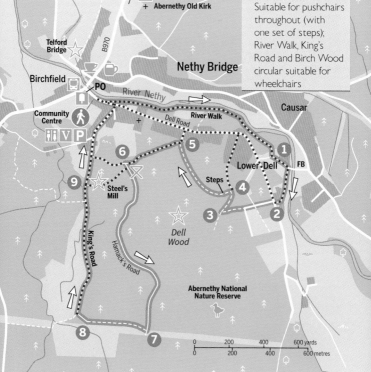

STORIES BEHIND THE WALK

☆ Telford Bridge

The three-arched stone bridge crossing the River Nethy in the middle of Nethy Bridge was designed by the famous Scottish engineer Thomas Telford, who designed roads, bridges, canals, dockyards and churches all over Britain. It opened in 1810 and replaced a singe-span bridge that had been washed away by a flood in the 1770s. Telford also designed the 15-span wooden bridge over the River Spey at nearby Broomhill.

☆ Dell Wood and Steel's Mill

In past centuries, Dell Wood, now part of Abernethy National Nature Reserve, was heavily exploited for timber. In 1855 a tree nursery was established to rear young pines from seeds collected in the forest for subsequent replanting. Two soaring non-native giant sequoias guard the entrance to the nursery. The shed at ⑨ is Steel's Mill and was used to produce kindling. It was built out of corrugated iron that came from a nearby World War I German Prisoner of War Camp.

Community Centre

River Walk

½ mile

➡ From Community Centre cross road and go **right** on Riverside Path.

➡ Ignore side path and stroll for almost ¾ mile to lane.

① ➡ Go **left** onto lane and walk past houses.

➡ Stay on lane where Lettoch Trail goes left over footbridge to reach T-junction.

② ➡ Go **straight over** road between redwood trees onto beech-hedged path.

➡ Keep **ahead** into mature pinewood for 300 yards to reach junction with big pine in the middle.

Castle Roy and Abernethy Old Kirk

Lying ¾ mile to the north of the village, Castle Roy is one of the oldest stone castles in Scotland, believed to date from the early 1200s. It was built by the Comyn family during the Norman colonisation of Scotland. The simple rectangular fortress has recently been restored and is open to visitors with all-abilities access. Beside the castle is Abernethy Old Kirk surrounded by an ancient graveyard. The current building dates from the early 1770s.

☆ Community Centre

Housed in the 1905 'Institute', the Community Centre provides meeting and recreational facilities for the local residents. It includes the Nethy Bridge Visitor Centre, which has fascinating exhibits and displays about the history and wildlife of the area. There is information about walking in Cairngorms National Park and details of the waymarked trails around the village.

1 mile   Steps   1½ miles

☆ Dell Wood

3 ➡ Turn **right** at junction and continue to next fork.

4 ➡ At post before track by white house, turn **left** downhill on rougher path through pines and down steps.
➡ Keep **forward** to next path junction.

5 ➡ Turn **left** at marker post where path joins from between houses on right.
➡ Walk on to next marker post.

NATURE NOTES

This walk visits a good variety of habitats, starting along the lively River Dulnain under broadleaved trees, where dog's mercury may be found, and across open areas with butterflies. Giant redwoods guard the entrance to Dell Wood, where the forest is dominated by Scots pine and associated plants, such as heather, blaeberry and cowberry. Look out for the beautiful angel's wings fungus on rotting wood.

Scots pine thrives on the well-drained but nutrient-poor soils of the Cairngorms. Its needles are joined in pairs, like a wishbone

Cowberry is a common plant of pine forests and is known as lingonberry in Scandinavia. It has little bell-shaped flowers and shiny, red berries

Hamack's Road

Dell Wood

6

2 miles

7

6 ➤ Here turn **left** (away from field on right) past picnic table.
➤ Keep **ahead** at next junction and follow path (Hamack's Road) for nearly ¾ mile to bench.

7 ➤ Stay on path as it makes pronounced **right** bend past bench in more open heathery area and then re-enters trees.
➤ Stroll 350 yards to bend marked by post and boulders.

Highland cattle are a hardy native breed that can live outside all year and in all weathers. They are relatively docile, despite the fearsome look of their horns, but cows can be very protective of their calves

The giant redwood (Wellingtonia) was introduced from North America in the 1850s. They can live for hundreds of years, so those in Scotland are only youngsters!

Angel's wings fungus is a white, bracket-like fungus that grows in clusters on decaying conifer wood. It is rare beyond the Highlands

King's Road   Steel's Mill ☆   Community Centre Ⅴ

2½ miles   3 miles   on B970, 🚌 🅿 150 yards 🚻

8 ➡ Bend **right** with path.
➡ Keep **right** at next post and in ⅓ mile look for sawmill information board on right.

9 ➡ Keep **ahead** past corrugated-iron shed on tarmac lane to main village street.
➡ Turn **left** along road back to Community Centre.

LOCH GARTEN AND LOCH MALLACHIE

Starting at RSPB Loch Garten reserve, this walk explores a forested part of Abernethy National Nature Reserve. It follows two waymarked trails: Big Pines, which runs under some of the oldest trees, and Two Lochs, which has views over both Loch Garten and smaller Loch Mallachie. Loch Garten is famous for ospreys, but the pine forest also provides habitat for many rare and endangered species, such as Scottish crossbill, crested tit, capercaillie, red squirrel, pine marten and twinflower. The forest has a thick understorey of juniper, rowan, birch, blaeberry and heather.

Distance	3.2 miles / 5.1 km
Time	1½ hours
Start/Finish	RSPB Loch Garten
Parking PH24 3BY	Loch Garten car park, signed from B970 between Boat of Garten and Nethy Bridge
Public toilets	At RSPB reception
Cafés/pubs	Hot drinks and snacks available from Nature Centre shop
Terrain	Well-made paths on the whole, but with two short rough-path sections
Hilliness	No hills; level throughout
Dogs	Dogs welcome. No stiles
Footwear	Year round

Did you know? The two lochs are crystal clear, but coloured brown because they are fed by peaty streams. The water is quite acidic, but supports a wide range of birdlife. Ducks include goldeneye, teal, wigeon and goosander, while whooper swans, greylag and pink-footed geese overwinter here.

Local legend According to tradition, Loch Garten was once frequented by the spirit of a Bodach (old man), who was feared in the surrounding countryside. He was occasionally seen as a spectre and his high-pitched screams filled people with dread because the sound heralded an impending death.

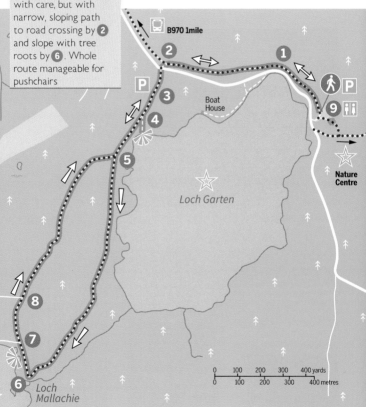

STORIES BEHIND THE WALK

☆ **Return of ospreys** Human persecution, especially by egg collectors, led to ospreys becoming extinct in Britain by the early 20th century. In 1954 a Scandinavian pair of birds nested at Loch Garten and the species slowly re-established. The RSPB purchased the reserve to protect wildlife and provide viewing opportunities for the public. The Nature Centre has hi-definition CCTV, binoculars and telescopes. Feeders outside are visited by red squirrels, bank voles and woodland birds.

🐦 Abernethy National Nature Reserve Loch Garten lies within a vast nature reserve that rises through forest and moorland to Britain's only subarctic montane plateau on the top of the Cairngorms. The reserve contains a wealth of wildlife with around 5,000 different species. Lochs Garten and Mallachie lie deep within the native Caledonian pinewood, a special habitat that once covered much of Scotland. Only 1 per cent is left, due to felling and overgrazing, and this is the largest area remaining.

☆ **Loch Garten**

(1 mile) ¦ ½ mile

P ➡ Take the path signed **Big Pines Trail**, on opposite side of car park from RSPB reception building.
➡ Stay on path through woods with 'granny' pines and understorey of juniper, heather and blaeberry.

1 ➡ Pass spot where people launch watercraft and continue on woodland path for 600 yards to reach sign and road.

2 ➡ At wooden Big Pines Trail sign (facing other way) cross road and keep **ahead** to small car park.

☆ **Historic timber felling** From 1728 the York Buildings Company used wood from Abernethy to make charcoal to smelt iron. During the Napoleonic Wars (1803–15) many pines were cut for ship building with the logs being floated down to the Spey via dams and cut channels. Timber from here helped to fuel the Industrial Revolution, being used for pit props, railway sleepers and even London's first water pipes. Some 300-year-old trees survive; they are often irregular, gnarled specimens that were not considered fit for timber.

☆ **Puggy Line**

During World War I a narrow-gauge railway was constructed by the Canadian Forestry Corps to carry timber from Abernethy Forest to Nethy Bridge. There was a sawmill there and a connection to the main railway line. Puggy is the nickname for the small steam engines used on this type of railway. It was closed after the war.

Loch Mallachie ☆

1 mile

④ ➤ At fork where arrow points right the walk continues this way, but first go **left** for view across Loch Garten to Bynack Mor.
➤ Return to Two Lochs Trail and go **left**. Walk to next junction.

1½ miles

③ ➤ Walk through car park and past Loch Mallachie information board onto **Two Lochs Trail**.

⑤ ➤ At next arrow fork **left** (right is the return route).
➤ Walk through forest to Loch Mallachie where path bends **right** at arrow.

NATURE NOTES

Loch Garten has all the wildlife of an ancient Caledonian pine forest, including rare species such as crested tits, creeping lady's tresses and twinflower. The understorey contains heather, juniper, blaeberry and cowberry. Other creatures use the lochs and wetlands, such as goldeneye ducks, damselflies and over-wintering geese and swans. Red squirrels and coal tits can be seen on the feeders at the nature centre.

Dead wood is a vital element of the woodland ecosystem. As insects and fungi break it down, nutrients are returned to the soil

Coal tits have a distinctive white patch at the back of their head, which other tits lack. They feed in conifers on insects and spiders, seeds and nuts

Blaeberry is the Scottish name for bilberry, meaning 'blue berry'

8

2 miles

6 ➥ Pass benches on path along shore. In bay, look for goldeneye nest box on dead tree standing in water.
➥ Follow path to next junction.

7 ➥ Keep **ahead** at end of bay where smaller path goes left along shore.
➥ Walk on to next path junction.

Creeping lady's tresses is a tiny, rare orchid only found in ancient pine forests

Juniper is one of Britain's native conifers, but a shrub rather than a tree. Its berries ripen from green to black and are used to flavour gin

RSPB Nature Centre ☆

2½ miles   P 🚻   3 miles   P

8 ➡ Ignore narrower path to the left and continue **ahead**.
➡ Bear **left** where you rejoin the outward trail and return through smaller car park.
➡ Cross road, rejoin Big Pines Trail and go **right** back to main car park.

9 ➡ Optionally, to visit RSPB Nature Centre, pay entry at reception building and follow marked path.

Opposite (clockwise): small pearl-bordered fritillary; male mallard duck; reindeer; osprey carving, Loch Garten; Scots pine bark
This page (clockwise): Highland cow; small heath butterfly; Scots pine cone

AVIEMORE TO BOAT OF GARTEN

The growth of both Aviemore and Boat of Garten was prompted by the construction of the railway to Forres in the 1860s. By 1892 a second line had been built to Inverness and Aviemore became an important junction. The town remains a stop on the mainline between Perth and Inverness. Trains provided easy access to the Highlands for tourists coming to enjoy the mountains and outdoor recreation, and many hotels were soon built. The Cairn Gorm ski area began to be developed in the 1960s leading to an expansion of Aviemore as a resort.

Distance	6 miles / 9.7 km
Time	2¾ hours
Start	Aviemore Station
Finish	Boat of Garten Station
Parking PH22 1RH	Speyside Railway car parks at Aviemore; PH24 3BH at Boat of Garten,
Public toilets	In Aviemore and Boat of Garten
Cafés/pubs	In Aviemore and Boat of Garten
Terrain	Pavements in towns and good paths in between; shared-use National Cycle Route 7
Hilliness	No hills; generally level with some short rises and dips
Dogs	Good for dogs but watch for bikes. No stiles
Footwear	Year round

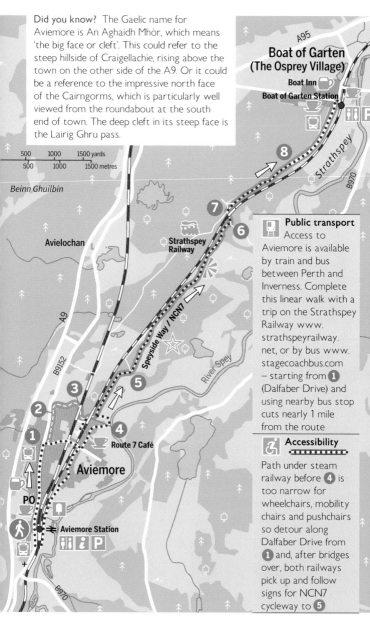

Did you know? The Gaelic name for Aviemore is An Aghaidh Mhòr, which means 'the big face or cleft'. This could refer to the steep hillside of Craigellachie, rising above the town on the other side of the A9. Or it could be a reference to the impressive north face of the Cairngorms, which is particularly well viewed from the roundabout at the south end of town. The deep cleft in its steep face is the Lairig Ghru pass.

Boat of Garten (The Osprey Village)

Boat Inn

Boat of Garten Station

A95

Strathspey

B970

Beinn Ghuilbin

500 1000 1500 yards
500 1000 1500 metres

Avielochan

Strathspey Railway

A9

B9152

Speyside Way / NCN7

River Spey

Route 7 Café

Aviemore

PO

Aviemore Station

B970

Public transport
Access to Aviemore is available by train and bus between Perth and Inverness. Complete this linear walk with a trip on the Strathspey Railway www.strathspeyrailway.net, or by bus www.stagecoachbus.com – starting from ❶ (Dalfaber Drive) and using nearby bus stop cuts nearly 1 mile from the route

Accessibility

Path under steam railway before ❹ is too narrow for wheelchairs, mobility chairs and pushchairs so detour along Dalfaber Drive from ❶ and, after bridges over, both railways pick up and follow signs for NCN7 cycleway to ❺

STORIES BEHIND THE WALK

☆ **Speyside Way** The Speyside Way is one of Scotland's official long-distance trails. It follows the River Spey upstream from near its mouth on the Moray coast via Aviemore to Newtonmore, a distance of 85 miles. Naturally, it can be walked in either direction and many of its sections make excellent day walks. The route between Aviemore and Boat of Garten follows the line of the Strathspey Railway, giving the chance of seeing steam trains chugging past.

 Strathspey Railway

The branch line from Aviemore to Forres was closed by the Beeching cuts in 1965, but in 1978 a dedicated group of volunteers formed the Strathspey Railway. This heritage railway has steam locomotives hauling vintage carriages with the option of dining on board. Today trains run for 10 miles between Aviemore and Nethy Bridge, via Boat of Garten, using the beautifully restored Victorian stations.

Aviemore Station

Craigellachie National Nature Reserve (distant left)

1 mile

➊ ➋

➤ With your back to Aviemore Station, go **right** on pavement past shops, pubs and cafés.

➤ Stay on pavement for nearly 1 mile to Dalfaber Drive.

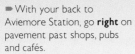

➊ ➤ At Dalfaber Drive turn **right** and go immediately **left** around metal railings onto tarmac path.

➤ Fork **left** and stay close to main road on path that becomes gravel to reach a crossing residential road.

🦆 Craigellachie National Nature Reserve

The steep, semi-wooded hillside rising to the west of Aviemore is a National Nature Reserve. It is a mixture of birch woodland, open glades and tree-fringed lochs. Peregrine falcons and buzzards may be seen here, plus a wealth of native wildflowers and insects such as the golden-ringed dragonfly. The reserve is entered via an A9 underpass by Aviemore Youth Hostel and has four waymarked trails.

☆ The Osprey Village

Boat of Garten is called the Osprey Village because it is where ospreys first nested after becoming extinct in Britain in the early 20th century. After a pair successfully bred at nearby Loch Garten in 1954, conservationists worked hard to protect local osprey nests from egg collectors. Slowly the numbers of this fish-eating bird of prey increased and there are now over 250 breeding pairs across Scotland.

Route 7 ☕ Café · · · · · 2 miles · · · · Speyside ☆ Way · · · · · 3 miles

2 ➡ Cross Dougal Drive and keep **ahead** at two fingerposts.
➡ Follow winding path to railway bridge, ignoring side paths to houses.

3 ➡ Pass through arch under railway and cross two footbridges.
➡ Keep **ahead** where path goes right to Dalfaber Industrial Estate, in dip cross footbridge and soon pass under second railway line on narrow path.

4 ➡ Meet National Cycle Route 7 (NCN7) merging from right and keep **ahead** on well-made path through birch and old pines.

NATURE NOTES

The habitats on this walk range from town fringes with wildflower-rich verges through lovely birch and pine woodland to open moorland. The wildlife to be seen changes through the seasons. In spring, woodland wildflowers such as wood sorrel bloom under the deciduous trees before they come into leaf. Many butterflies flit about in summer and bearberry flowers amid the heather. Hazel nuts and other seeds ripen in autumn, while in winter geese fly overhead and hazel catkins develop.

Birch trees have small, diamond-shaped leaves and white bark with dark fissures. They shed seed from their catkins in spring

Hazel catkins

Strathspey Railway

3 miles

4 miles

5 ➡ At NCN7 post bend **left** into more open heathery ground with many young pines.
➡ Continue for 1½ miles to gate with views right to Cairngorm mountains.

6 ➡ Beyond gate turn **left** on stony track signed Boat of Garten 1½ miles.
➡ Go over cattle grid, under rail bridge and up a slope where track merges from left.

Hazel bushes tend to have many stems. Pollen from catkins, the male flowers, fertilise tiny red female flowers that develop into nuts

Wood sorrel has delicate white flowers and fresh green clover-shaped leaves

Red admiral butterflies may be seen from spring to autumn

Boat of Garten Station

The Osprey Village ☆

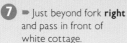

5 miles

6 miles

7 ➥ Just beyond fork **right** and pass in front of white cottage.
➥ After ¾ mile walk through open gateway to join road.

8 ➥ Keep **ahead** up tarmac, past 30 mph sign, into Boat of Garten.
➥ At end of Kinchurdy Road, opposite Village Shop, turn **right** then go **right** beyond Boat Inn to Strathspey Railway.

LOCH MORLICH

Loch Morlich is a glacial feature known as a kettle hole, a hollow where a large body of ice persisted as the glaciers that gouged the north face of the Cairngorms retreated about 10,000 years ago. This walk starts near Glenmore Forest Park Visitor Centre and takes you through peaceful pinewoods with beautiful views over the water. It returns along the Old Logging Way, an off-road route whose name reflects the historic use of Glenmore for forestry.

Distance	3.6 miles / 5.8 km
Time	1¾ hours
Start/Finish	Glenmore
Parking PH22 1QU	Loch Morlich Beach car park
Public toilets	Loch Morlich Beach, just after start
Cafés/pubs	Cafés at Boathouse on beach and 500 yards along the lane at Glenmore Visitor Centre and Glenmore Shop
Terrain	Forest paths and tracks
Hilliness	Level throughout
Dogs	Dogs welcome under close control or on leads. No stiles
Footwear	Winter 🥾 Spring/Summer/ Autumn 👟

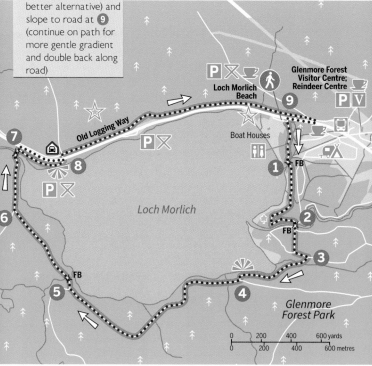

Did you know? During World War II a company of Norwegian soldiers, known as Kompani Linge, trained in Glenmore Forest and the mountains. The terrain helped them prepare for commando raids into Nazi-occupied Norway, during which 57 of them died. A Norwegian flag flies in their memory.

Local legend Loch Morlich was said to be guarded by the Spectre of the Bloody Hand – a gigantic figure of an old man, in Highland warrior dress, one hand dripping with blood. He was a champion of animals, being a guardian of deer and other wild creatures. But he challenged any human he met to fight to the death.

Glenmore Forest Visitor Centre; Reindeer Centre

Loch Morlich Beach

Old Logging Way

Boat Houses

Loch Morlich

Glenmore Forest Park

0   200   400   600 yards
0   200   400   600 metres

STORIES BEHIND THE WALK

☆ **Loch Morlich beach** Loch Morlich is famed for having the highest beach in Britain, at 1,050 feet above sea level. There are actually some higher lochs with beaches, but none with such a vast stretch of sand. The coarse red sand is made of eroded granite, which has been washed down from the Cairngorm mountains over millions of years.

☆ **Cairngorm ski resort**
The ski resort on Cairngorm, Scotland's sixth highest mountain, is visible from Loch Morlich beach. It is 10 miles from Glenmore and is on the bus service from Aviemore. As well as being a major snow sports centre with many lifts and runs, it has panoramic views back over Glenmore and Loch Morlich. In summer it is a popular start point for hill walking and climbing.

☆ Loch Morlich beach

½ mile

➤ At bottom of car park, follow path with marker post past wooden toilet block.
➤ Pass bench at top of big sandy beach and continue to a footbridge.

1 ➤ Cross bridge and walk parallel to loch shore under big old pines with campsite on left.
➤ Path runs on to meet river and swings **left** beside it to another footbridge.

☆ Restoring native woodlands

The original woodland cover around the Cairngorms was Scots pine-dominated forest, with juniper, birch, rowan, aspen and alder trees adding colour and variety. Past management has seen the creation of large plantations of introduced conifers that are more uniform and poorer for wildlife. On this walk you will see a large area where diseased, non-native lodgepole pine have been felled and native woodland is being restored.

☆ **Reindeer Centre** A free-ranging herd of reindeer live in the Cairngorms, the only place in Britain with the subarctic mountain tundra habitat they need. Guided hill walks from the Reindeer Centre in Glenmore take visitors to the mountainside to see them. They are tame and can be hand fed. A small group, regularly alternated with those on the hill, can be visited in paddocks at the centre. At Christmas several depart to pull Santa's sleigh.

---

4 ▪▪
⌐ 1 mile   ⌐ 1½ miles

2 ▪ Turn **right** over bridge and keep **ahead**.
▪ Shortly after, fork **right** and at next fork go **left**. Walk 100 yards to next junction.

3 ▪ At this third fork after bridge, go **right** on path through wet woodland.
▪ Loch comes into view again. Continue to some handily placed seats with loch views.

4 ▪ Beyond benches turn **right** at T-junction along track.
▪ Walk for ¾ mile to a wide junction. Keep **right** here.

NATURE NOTES

Set at over 1,000 feet (305m) at the foot of
the Cairngorm mountains, Loch Morlich can
be a harsh environment in winter. Some hardy
wildlife can survive here all year, including
reindeer, roe deer and the Scottish crossbill.
Other species, such as mallard ducks, move to
lower, less ice-locked areas in winter. Many
wildflowers survive underground as roots or
seeds and re-emerge in the spring.

One-flowered
wintergreen, also
called St Olaf's
Candlestick, is only
found in pine
forests in
north-east
Scotland. It has a
single nodding
white flower and a
rosette of leaves
at the base

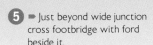

2 miles   2½ miles

5 ➡ Just beyond wide junction
cross footbridge with ford
beside it.
➡ Keep **ahead** for 500 yards
to forest road junction.

6 ➡ Beyond green barrier meet
forest road and turn **right**
along it.
➡ Cross vehicle bridge over
outflow from loch.

The beak of the Scottish crossbill is twisted, with the two halves not meeting neatly. It has evolved this way to enable them to prise seeds out of pine cones. Colourful like small parrots, the males are orange-red and the females yellowish-green

Roe deer are widespread across all of Scotland, but need woodland for shelter. Their summer coats are a rich red-brown, but they turn grey-brown in winter

Glenmore Forest Visitor Centre and Reindeer Centre (500 yards)

☆ Old Logging Way

P ✕ 3 miles

7 ➠ Immediately go **right** on path by water and into car park, by small beach (picnic benches and views over loch to mountains).

8 ➠ By walks information board in car park turn **left**, cross road with care then go **right** along Old Logging Way path.
➠ Keep to this for 1 mile to return to Morlich Beach car park.

🚌 **V** **9** 3½ miles

9 ➠ For the visitor centre (car park) and other Glenmore Forest attractions continue on path for 500 yards.
➠ To conclude walk, pass above car park then turn sharp **right** on path that angles back down to road and cross by entrance.

P 🏠 ☕ ✕

WALK 7 CATCH A BUS

DALRADDY TO KINCRAIG

This walk runs between the River Spey and the mainline railway. Initially it has wide views over open pasture to the Cairngorm mountains. Beyond the little settlement of Speybank you enter woods that include beautiful stands of aspen, a tree that is rare outside the Highlands. The path runs high above the river with glimpses of wild land on the other side, where the River Feshie meets the Spey. Otters and ospreys frequent the river and the trees are alive with woodland birds. Check bus timetables (see opposite) before setting out, or stroll as far you feel like then retrace your outward route.

Distance
2.9 miles / 4.7 km

Time
1½ hours

Start
Dalraddy Holiday Park, Alvie

Finish
Kincraig

Parking PH22 1QB
Dalraddy Holiday Park car park – signed off B9152 along Holiday Park access drive; go left into car park before barrier to Holiday Park

Public toilets
None

Cafés/pubs
Alvie Forest Food at start, Old Post Office Café and Suie Bar in Kincraig

Did you know? Kincraig was originally called Boat of Insh, because a ferry crossed the River Spey here. That was also the name given to the station when the railway arrived in 1863. Eight years later a bridge was built to replace the ferry and the railway company renamed it Kincraig.

Local legend The parish church on the shore of Loch Insh, just beyond Kincraig Bridge, is dedicated to St Adamnan (c625–704), the biographer of St Columba. It contains an ancient bronze bell that dates from his time and is believed to have healing powers.

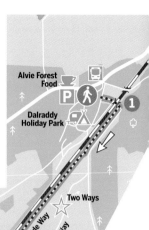

Alvie Forest Food

Dalraddy Holiday Park

Two Ways

Speyside Way

Badenoch Way

Dalraddy Moor

B9152

A9

Speybank

River Spey

River Feshie

200   400   600 yards
200   400   600 metres

Terrain
Well-surfaced path, with some muddy track sections; pavement

Hilliness
Mostly level, but between **5** and **7** there are some short, steep dips and rises

Dogs
Good walk for dogs. No stiles

Footwear
Winter
Spring/Summer/Autumn

Public transport
Complete the walk with a three-minute bus journey. Services operated by Scottish Citylink www.citylink.co.uk and Stagecoach Highlands www.stagecoachbus.com

Accessibility
Whole route suitable for pushchairs, but short, sharp dips and rises between **5** and **7** possibly too steep for wheelchairs

STORIES BEHIND THE WALK

☆ **Highland Wildlife Park** Scotland's only polar bears live just south of Kincraig (2 miles down the B9152) at Highland Wildlife Park. It is home to over 200 animals, including wolves, snow leopards and Arctic foxes. Owned by the Royal Zoological Society of Scotland, the park makes an exciting day out. Visitors can drive through large paddocks with deer, elk, bison and wild horses and walk around the central area with numerous enclosures for individual species.

☆ **Alvie and Dalraddy Estate**
Dalraddy Holiday Park is part of a larger estate that includes farmland, forest and Loch Alvie. The start car park is the base for Cairngorm Archery and Cairngorm Quad Treks, which take groups out on quad bikes. Other recreational activities available on the estate include fishing, horse riding, gorge walking and whizzing down zip wires.

Dalraddy Holiday Park ☆ **Two Ways**

| | 1/2 mile |

Alvie Forest Food

➡ Leave car park by gate on far side and keep **ahead** on track that soon goes under railway.

1 ➡ Immediately beyond arch turn **right** on Speyside Way, signed 'Kincraig 2¾ miles'.
➡ Walk beside railway, with view over field on left to Cairngorm mountains, to gate in ¾ mile.

2 ➡ Go through gate and keep **ahead** on track into wood, eventually to reach another gate.

☆ Kincraig and Loch Insh

Just to the left of where the Speybank path meets the road in Kincraig ⑧ is the popular Old Post Office Café, which is also a colourful gallery. Another refreshments stop is Loch Insh Watersports Centre, a mile away on the east shore of Loch Insh. The loch has ducks, geese, swans and a pair of osprey often nest on an island at the north end. A gate near ⑧ leads to the shore if you want a closer look.

☆ Two Ways

This walk uses a relatively new section of the Speyside Way, one of Scotland's official long-distance trails that follows the course of the River Spey for 85 miles. Along the way you will see some signs for the older Badenoch Way, a route between Dalraddy and Kingussie. It is a narrower, rougher path that runs closer to the river and intersects in several places with the wider, better-surfaced Speyside Way.

☆ Alvie and Dalraddy Estate

────②──────────────┼──────────③──────────────④────
                1 mile ┆

④ ⮞ Where road bends right over railway, go straight **ahead** through gate on Speyside Way, signed 'Kincraig 1¼ miles'.
⮞ Pass bench with view over River Spey and stay on gravel-surfaced path to reach wooden barrier.

③ ⮞ Exit wood through gate.
⮞ Track runs past houses of Speybank and becomes tarmac road.

NATURE NOTES

Views on this walk extend over Glen Feshie, a wild area on the other side of the River Spey, to the eastern flank of the Cairngorm mountains. If you are lucky you might see an otter fishing in the river below. Sheep often graze the open pasture near the start. After going through a pine plantation you are into native deciduous woodland where the star species is aspen, a tree that is scarce in most of the UK.

The leaves of oak trees are eaten by a whole host of insects. Squirrels, jays and badgers love their acorns. There are 326 species of wildlife that only live on oak

Lichen

4 ·········· **5**
1½ miles · 2 miles

5 ➥ Under a grove of tall aspen walk round barrier then zigzag down into dip and up other side past another barrier.

6 ➥ In next dip cross footbridge over stream and stay on main path, which bends **left** where grass path runs ahead.
➥ At next bend fork **right**.

Birch polypore fungus grows on birch trunks and is also called razor strop fungus because it can be used to sharpen knives

Fly agaric

The scientific name of aspen, *Populus tremula*, gives a clue to its distinctive character. Because the round leaves are borne on long, slim stalks they tremble in the slightest breeze, giving a shimmering appearance and creating a rustling sound

Kincraig and Loch Insh ☆

Highland Wildlife Park (2 miles) ☆

2½ miles

Old Post Office Café

3 miles

Kincraig

7 ➡ Where path rises to meet track go **left** along Speyside Way, signed 'Kincraig ¼ mile'.
➡ Continue on Speyside Way (named Speybank Walk) as far as road junction.

8 ➡ Turn **right** on meeting road onto The Brae (Old Post Office Café is 100 yards to **left**).
➡ Walk **uphill** and under railway and keep **ahead** to main road.

9 ➡ At T-junction by war memorial turn **right** along B9152 for 20 yards to bus stop.

Opposite (clockwise): Cairngorm Hotel, Aviemore; Joe's Chippy, Kingussie. This page (clockwise): Boat House Cafe, Loch Morlich; Clootie dumpling, Loch Garten; Farm shop and Barn, Rothiemurchus, Loch an Eilein; Toshac's Tuck Shop, Newtonmore; Nethy House Cafe and Rooms, Nethy Bridge.

LOCH AN EILEIN

Loch an Eilein (Gaelic for 'loch of the island') is one of the most beautiful locations in Cairngorms National Park. Native Caledonian pinewood surrounds the water and on still days the trees create magical reflections. The ruins of an ancient castle stand on the loch's one island and the woods are rich in wildlife. This peaceful spot feels hidden away although it is only three miles south of Aviemore. You'll want to linger, so bring a picnic and make a day of your visit.

Distance	3.5 miles/5.6 km
Time	1¾ hours
Start/Finish	Loch an Eilein, signed off B970 1 mile south of Inverdruie
Parking PH22 1QP	Loch an Eilein car park (charge)
Public toilets	Behind cottage near ❶
Cafés/pubs	Nearest in Inverdruie
Terrain	Forest paths and tracks
Hilliness	Fairly level with only slight gradients
Dogs	Dogs welcome under close control or on leads. No stiles
Footwear	Year round 🥾

Public transport
None

Accessibility
••••••••••

Fully pushchair
accessible. For
wheelchairs, **1** to **6**
some path surfaces
are uneven and may
not be suitable

Did you know? In past centuries many more
people lived and worked in the forest, harvesting
trees and growing crops in small fields. Cut
timber was dragged by pony to the loch, where
sluices controlled the outflow. When released the
water floated the logs down Milton Burn to the
Spey. A grain mill once stood where the car park
is now and stone ruins near **1** are the remains
of a lime-burning kiln, which was in use until 1876.

Local legend Loch an Eilein Castle is reputed to
have been a stronghold of the infamous Wolf
of Badenoch, Andrew Stewart, who sacked and
burned Forres and Elgin in 1390.

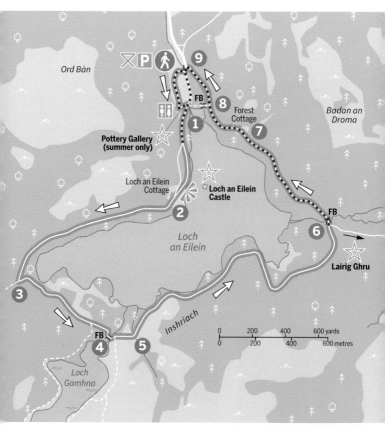

STORIES BEHIND
THE WALK

☆ **Loch an Eilein Castle** The origins of the castle are lost in the mists of time, but historians believe it is at least 600 years old. In 1690 Jacobite troops attacked it while retreating from the Battle of Cromdale, but were fought off by the women, children and old folk sheltering there. It is said that a zigzag causeway once linked the island to the shore, but was submerged when the water level was raised by a dam.

☆ **Thieves' Road** A historic route used by cattle raiders ran between Loch an Eilein and adjoining Loch Gamhna. It was used by clansmen from more mountainous areas who descended on the fertile lands of Strathspey to steal livestock. Loch Gamhna means 'Loch of the Stirks' (young cattle) and it was here that locals tied a few cows to a tree in the hope that their main herds would be spared.

Pottery Gallery ☆ (summer only)

Loch an Eilein Castle

¡ ½ mile

➡ Walk out of far end of car park past Rothiemurchus Forest sign.

➡ Turn **left** by the white cottage and toilets to the loch shore.

1 ➡ Facing the loch turn **right** on track for an anticlockwise circuit.

➡ Fork **left** at junction (Loch an Eilein cottage signed to right) to gate.

2 ➡ Pass through gate in stone wall.

➡ Follow path under granny pines to signpost at west end of loch.

☆ Rothiemurchus Estate

Extending to about 40 square miles, Rothiemurchus is a large private estate that has been owned by the Grant family for almost 500 years. It lies at the heart of Cairngorms National Park and is managed for nature and people. The Estate has a Farm Shop and The Barn café at Inverdruie and offers a wide range of outdoor activities from quad biking to feeding red deer.

☆ **Lairig Ghru** This famous pass is visible from a distance as a deep cleft in the steep north face of the Cairngorm mountains. The route links Strathspey to Deeside and involves at least 19 miles of tough walking between the nearest roads at either end. A large boulder on the south side of the boulder-strewn pass is called the Tailors' Stone (Clach nan Taillear) in memory of three drunken tailors who perished trying to shelter from a violent storm one Hogmanay.

Loch Gamhna ☆

3 ——— **4** — **5**

¦ 1 mile   1½ miles ¦

3 ➤ At 'path' sign turn **left**.
➤ Keep **left** where 'path not maintained' marked on right and walk to footbridge.

4 ➤ Cross bridge over outflow from Loch Gamhna.
➤ Keep **ahead** at another 'path not maintained' marked on right and continue to next bridge.

5 ➤ Swing **left** over burn then walk 1 mile to gate at track junction.
➤ Through gate, keep **ahead** where Lairig Ghru path is signed to right to reach footbridge.

NATURE NOTES

On this walk you stroll under some enormous, rugged Scots pines that are more than 300 years old. These hoary old trees often survived felling because they were heavily branched or irregular in shape. They are known as 'granny pines' because the younger generations of trees around them have sprouted from their seed.

The green-veined white butterfly frequents wilder, damper environments than the familiar 'cabbage whites'

Red deer use the forest for shelter and feeding. During the autumn rut the roars of stags echo around the glens

2 miles

2½ miles

6 ➤ Cross bridge and follow track as it swings **left**.
➤ Continue to gate in 600 yards.

7 ➤ Go through gate and past red-painted Forest Cottage.
➤ Walk to next junction near north end of loch.

Hard fern remains green for most of the year. It has two types of frond; the spore-bearing ones grow in the middle and are longer, narrower and upright

Capercaillie is a large grouse of pine woodland. It was reintroduced in Victorian times after going extinct in Britain, but it is again endangered

Great tits are woodland birds

☆ Path to Lairig Ghru

━━━━━⑥▪▪▪▪▪▪▪▪▪▪▪▪▪▪▪▪▪⑦▪▪▪▪▪▪▪▪⑧▪▪▪▪⑨▪━━

3 miles   3½ miles   P

                                                   ✕

⑧ ➡ At red sign (facing other way at junction) keep **ahead** to barrier. (Toilets to left, over footbridge.)

⑨ ➡ Go round barrier to road end and turn **left** over bridge to car park.

GO BY TRAIN
CATCH A BUS

KINGUSSIE

Kingussie is a planned town, built by the 4th Duke of Gordon in the 1790s. The original settlement was on the other side of the Spey at Ruthven, where old roads came together at a ford across the river. The first part of this walk is there-and-back to historic Ruthven Barracks. The second part follows the Gynack Mill Trail around a wooded stream where there are several interpretation boards about the history of the place.

Distance	
3.6 miles/5.7km	
Time	
2 hours	
Start/Finish	
Kingussie	
Parking PH21 1EU	
Ardvonie car park	
Public toilets	
Ardvonie car park	
Cafés/pubs	
Kingussie	
Terrain	
Good paths and road to Ruthven Barracks; road and earth paths with steps around Gynack Burn	
Hilliness	
Fairly flat except for short climb to top of Ruthven Barracks mound and undulations on Gynack Mill Trail	
Dogs	
Dogs welcome under close control or on leads. No stiles	
Footwear	
Year round	

Public transport

Kingussie lies on mainline railway between Inverness and Perth with other stations up the line at Aviemore and Carrbridge and down the line at Newtonmore and Dalwhinnie. If travelling by train, join walk at ❶. Bus stops in Kingussie on Newtonmore Road (A86) with services operating from Newtonmore via Kingussie to Aviemore www. stagecoachbus.com

Accessibility

Wheelchairs/ pushchair accessible on path/road to foot of Ruthven Barracks, where there is a kissing-gate; steps and steeper slopes on Gynack Mill Trail not suitable for wheelchairs

Did you know? Traditionally sturdy Highland ponies were the workhorses of Badenoch. They have been bred for over 150 years by the Ormiston family, who now use them for riding treks and holidays. Their centre is beside the railway station and you are bound to see some of the ponies grazing around Ruthven.

Did you know? Robert Louis Stevenson, the famous Scottish author, spent holidays in Kingussie in the 1880s. In a poem he called the Gynack his 'Golden Burn'. He loved sailing paper boats on it and imagining them being found by other children 'a hundred miles or more' downstream.

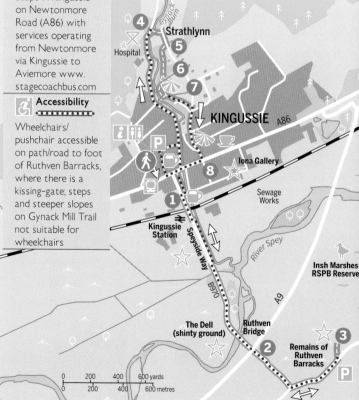

STORIES BEHIND
THE WALK

☆ **Ruthven Barracks** Over the centuries there have been several castles on the natural mound at Ruthven, including a wooden one built in 1229. Ruthven Barracks was constructed in 1719 by General Wade, who was tasked with controlling the rebellious clans after the first Jacobite uprising. It was connected by military roads with three other identical infantry garrisons. In 1745 government troops were forced to surrender after being besieged by 300 Highlanders who then set fire to the barracks.

🐦 Insh Marshes RSPB Reserve
From Ruthven Barracks there is a splendid view over Insh Marshes. The parking and trails around the RSPB Reserve are another ¾ mile along the Speyside Way. Part of the Spey's natural flood plain, the marshes are one of the most important wetlands in Europe for birds, wildflowers and insects.

Duke of
🍽 Gordon Hotel   The Dell
                  ☆ Speyside Way   (shinty ground) ☆

🅿   🍽 Silverfjord   ½ mile
     Hotel
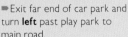

➊ ▸Exit far end of car park and turn **left** past play park to main road.
▸Go **left** and opposite Duke of Gordon Hotel cross road to walk through park, then go **right** to crossroads by Silverfjord Hotel.

➊ ▸Turn **left** to follow road over level-crossing then take Speyside Way path beside road.
▸Rejoin road, pass The Dell and cross Ruthven Bridge over River Spey.

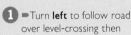

☆ The Dell

Shinty, in Gaelic Camanachd, is an ancient Celtic sport that looks to the uninitiated like a violent form of hockey! It is a fast-moving and highly skilful game that is a popular spectator sport in the Highlands. The Dell is the Kingussie team's playing ground. There are five clubs in the Cairngorms, including Newtonmore and Kincraig, but Kingussie have won the national league most often.

☆ **Iona Gallery** Kingussie has a lively community with many different societies. The Iona Gallery is run by Badenoch & Strathspey Artists whose membership is drawn from artists and craftspeople across the area. Entry is free to the changing exhibitions that portray local life and scenery. The gallery has a full programme of events, with workshops and community events in winter.

Ruthven Barracks ☆ 🦆 Insh Marshes RSPB Reserve (½ mile)

❸

🅿

mile

1½ miles

❷ ➡ Walk under A9 flyover and **uphill** on road, bending **left** at a junction.
➡ Continue to Ruthven Barracks and kissing-gate at foot of path to ruins.

❸ ➡ After visit, return by outward route to Ardvonie car park.
➡ From vehicle entrance walk **left** up Gynack Road for over ½ mile to picnic tables and walks board.

NATURE NOTES

The steep little valley of the Gynack Burn is shaded by native deciduous woodland that is rich in wildlife. In spring it is carpeted in wildflowers, such as wood anemone, wood sorrel and primrose. In autumn red squirrels can be seen overhead in the hazels, looking for nuts. A very different habitat is found across the Spey at the foot of Ruthven Barracks, where the Insh Marshes are home to redshank, lapwing and oystercatcher.

Red squirrels thrive in the Cairngorms, where they eat the seeds from pine cones and have no competition from grey squirrels

It's hard to miss the giant funnel fungus, with its whitish colour and large, cornucopia-shaped cap

2 miles   2½ miles

4 ▸Turn **right** over footbridge; go **right** to Grampian Sanatorium board and **left** up steps.
▸Turn **right** along road for 100 yards to fingerpost and gate.

5 ▸Turn **right** on fenced path that bends into wood then turn **right** beyond 'Woods with a past' board.
▸Descend to viewpoint seat above burn by Robert Louis Stevenson board.

6 ▸Continue to Duke's Town board just before a footbridge.
▸Don't cross but turn sharp **left** on path up steps to fingerpost.

Highland ponies have been bred to carry loads over rough ground without tiring or stumbling. Now they are often used for trekking

Rowan, also called mountain ash, is often planted by houses to ward off evil spirits

Creeping thistle is considered an agricultural weed, but its flowers are an important source of nectar for bumblebees, butterflies and other insects

Clock Tower

Iona Gallery (300 yards)

4 5 6 7 8

3 miles

3½ miles

P

fff

i

7 ➤Turn **right** through gate and **right** again on meeting tarmac lane.
➤Descend past viewpoint by clock tower (left) to reach main road.

8 ➤At crossroads turn **right** along main road, cross bridge over burn and turn **right** up Gynack Road back to car park.

WALK 10

NEWTONMORE

This walk follows the flatter half of the Wildcat Trail, which circuits Newtonmore. The route runs along the banks of two rivers: the Calder, which drains Glen Banchor, and the Spey, which it flows into. As the path is on the floodplain, parts may be underwater and impassable when these rivers are in spate. The meadows fill with wildflowers in summer when the high-pitched peeps of breeding sandpipers can be heard along the riverbanks.

Distance	4.5 miles/7.2km
Time	2¼ hours
Start/Finish	Newtonmore
Parking PH20 1DZ	Glen Road car park
Public toilets	In Main Street, beside Wildcat Trail shop
Cafés/pubs	In Main Street
Terrain	Pavement, road verge and narrow grass/earth riverside path
Hilliness	Flat with some short slopes up and down
Dogs	Dogs welcome. Several stiles to cross
Footwear	Winter 🥾 Spring/Autumn 🥾 👟 Summer 👟

Public transport

Newtonmore lies on mainline railway between Inverness and Perth with other stations between Carrbridge and Dalwhinnie. If travelling by train, join walk at ❶.
Bus stops in Main Street (A86) with services operating to Newtonmore from Dalwhinnie and Aviemore, www. stagecoachbus.com

Accessibility

Start to ❷ (Main Street, Station Road and Laggan Road) accessible to wheelchairs and pushchairs, and ❽ to route end, but riverside path is too narrow and uneven, with several stiles

Did you know? In the past, Loch Imrich was used as a curling pond and skating rink in winter. Today it is a tranquil wildlife walk, right in the heart of the village.

Local legend It is believed that the sport of shinty originated in Ireland, and was brought across the sea to Scotland around 2,000 years ago, along with Christianity and the Gaelic language. The game developed differently in the two countries, becoming hurling in Ireland. A 15th-century warrior's tombstone found on Iona bore the carving of a shinty stick and ball along with his broadsword. Newtonmore's shinty ground, the Eilan, is near ❸.

Walk 10 Newtonmore 75

STORIES BEHIND THE WALK

☆ **River Spey** The Spey is one of the largest, least polluted and unmodified river systems in Britain. As it meanders, the position of shingle banks and pools changes constantly. Between ④ and ⑤ you can see how it is eroding the slope opposite. The river has conservation status to protect four key species: salmon, sea lamprey, otter and the freshwater pearl mussel.

☆ Wildcats
The wildcat has long been the symbol of Newtonmore, as Clan Chattan, a confederation of local clans, uses the wildcat as its crest. Wildcats look like domestic tabby cats with a sturdy build and distinctive bushy tail marked by bold black rings. The species is on the brink of extinction in Scotland and a programme is underway to breed animals in captivity and release them to the wild to bolster the remaining population.

Clan Macpherson Museum

River ☆ Calder

①

| ½ mile

②

| 1 mil

➡ From car park, walk down Glen Road to junction; turn **right** past Newtonmore Hall and walk the length of Main Street.
➡ At a fork keep **left** past Glen Hotel (on left) and Clan Macpherson Museum (on right) to crossroads beyond Esso garage.

(600 yards)

① ➡ Turn **right** up Station Road then turn **left** along A86 (narrow pavement on right side).
➡ Continue to just before road bridge (last 250 yards on grassy verge).

② ➡ Branch **left** down tarmac ramp to a wooden pedestrian gate beside a metal field gate.
➡ Follow path downstream by River Calder, go over stile and continue to Spey Bridge.

Clan Macpherson Museum

This museum opened in 1952 and contains a large collection of historical artefacts with rooms set out to reflect different periods. A visit gives insight into the clan system and roles of various members of the Macpherson Clan, whose chiefs are known as Macpherson of Cluny. The house was built in 1908 and has starred as both a post office and a tearoom in the TV series *Monarch of the Glen*.

Highland Folk Museum

This living history museum brings to life the domestic and working conditions of earlier Highland peoples. Many traditional exhibits have been rescued and rebuilt in a large 80-acre site, with different areas representing various eras. Costumed actors show what life was like and demonstrate crafts to visitors.

☆ River Spey

1½ miles

2 miles

3 ➤ Pass under concrete road bridge.
➤ Cross two stiles beside metal gates by caravan park and follow river to rail bridge.

4 ➤ Pass under railway and go through kissing-gate.
➤ Bend **left** with riverside path and continue to next kissing-gate.

5 ➤ Keep **ahead** through the gate and climb over stile where Coffin Road signed to left.
➤ Continue by river, through gate and along field edge to where grassy path signed to station.

NATURE NOTES

Quite different in character to other walks, this route takes you close to the dynamic River Spey, which creates its own special environment. You will walk under alder trees, which can survive regular flooding. Some plants, such as Michaelmas daisy, are probably carried here by the river. The path crosses open grassland full of wildflowers, including Devil's-bit scabious, wood cranesbill and dog rose.

The lilac-blue flowers of **Devil's-bit scabious** look like little pin cushions. They grow in damp meadows and attract a wide variety of insects

Michaelmas daisy has established itself in the wild along riverbanks and loch shores. It flowers late summer/early autumn

Golf
⚠ course   ☆ **River Spey**   **7**

2½ miles   3 miles

6 ➡ Here, keep **ahead** over two stiles and stay on path for more than ½ mile to footbridge.
➡ On the way, pass along edge of golf course then across grassland and under trees where stepping stones cross wet ground.

7 ➡ Cross footbridge and walk between stream and fence.
➡ Go over railway bridge, pass water treatment works to junction where paths lead into Highland Folk Museum on both sides.